D1391362

RU

KITCHENS
Through the Ages

Richard Wood

WAYLAND

Editor: Jason Hook
Book design: Simon Borrough
Series design: Ian Winton
Cover design: Dennis Day

First published in 1997 by Wayland Publishers Ltd, 61 Western Road, Hove,
East Sussex, BN3 1JD, England

Find Wayland on the internet at http://www.wayland.co.uk

British Library Cataloguing in Publication Data
Wood, Richard, 1949-
Kitchens through the ages. - (Rooms through the ages)
1. Kitchens - History - Juvenile literature 2. Social history
- Juvenile literature
I. Title II. De Saulles, Tony
643.3'09

ISBN 0 7502 2059 7

Printed and bound by G. Canale & CsPA, Turin, Italy

Cover pictures: (Main picture) An electric cooker and fuseboard, 1912. (Background) A banquet
shown on a medieval manuscript. Title page: Chefs shown on a medieval manuscript.

Picture Acknowledgements: The publishers would like to thank the following for permission to
reproduce their pictures: Bridgeman Art Library 21(left), /Chicago Press, USA 6(top), /Fitzwilliam
Museum, University of Cambridge 6(bottom), /Glastonbury Abbey, Somerset 14(bottom), /British
Library, London 15(top), /Private Collection 15(bottom), 18, /Pushkin Museum, Moscow 16,
/National Gallery of Scotland, Edinburgh 20(top), /Christopher Wood Gallery, London 23(bottom),
/Formica Ltd, North Shields 29(top); British Library *cover* (background), 1, 12, 13; British Museum
7(left), 8(top), 10(bottom), 14(top); C.M. Dixon 4(top), 5(top), 7(right), 9(right); Werner Forman
Archive 5(bottom); Habitat 29(bottom); Robert Harding 22(left); Hulton Getty 20(bottom),
27(bottom), 28(bottom); Museum of London 8(bottom); National Trust 17(top), 19(bottom),
23(top), 26(bottom); Norfolk Museums Service 4(bottom), 22(right), 25(bottom); Robert Opie
24(top), 25(top), 25(centre); Popperfoto 24(bottom); Reading Museum Service 11(bottom); Science
and Society *cover* (main picture), 21(right); Wayland Picture Library 9(left), 19(top), 27(top),
28(top); Richard Wood 17(bottom), 26(top); York Archaeological Trust 10(top), 11(top).
All artwork by Tony de Saulles.

CONTENTS

Stone Age Stews

Very Fast Food

The first humans could not pop into a shop for a burger. Their favourite 'fast food' ran past on four legs! Prehistoric people hunted animals, birds and fish, and gathered fruits and nuts. Nobody knows when they first used 'kitchens'. It may have been half a million years ago. We do know that some foods, such as barnacles, taste terrible uncooked.

▲ Stone Age cooks used ovens like this.

▼ Stone Age tools for catching and preparing food.

Prehistoric cooks hung mammoth steaks by the fire to roast. They cooked other foods in animal-skin 'pots' filled with water. Stones were heated in the fire until they were red-hot, then dropped into the water until it boiled – an ingenious idea.

The Seed of an Idea

'We plough the fields and scatter the good seed on the land,' says a famous hymn. People have not always known how to do this. It was along the fertile rivers of the Middle East that people first discovered how to farm crops. The idea only reached Britain and northern Europe about 5,000 years ago. The first crops were wheat-like grasses called 'einkhorn' and 'emmer'. Our modern types of grain were developed over many centuries, as people mixed wild varieties together.

▲ Women used this quern and rubbing stone to grind grain into flour.

FANCY THAT!

Bread Source
Prehistoric people had unusual bread ovens. They dropped a hot rock into a hole in the ground, placed loaves on it, then covered the hole with twigs and earth to keep in the heat.

TASTY TITBITS

Celtic Cooks
A historian described Celtic people in about 50 BC: 'Beside them are hearths blazing with fire, with cauldrons and spits containing large pieces of meat. They honour their bravest warriors with the finest portions of the meat.'

▼ These stones at Skara Brae, in the Orkneys, formed a 5,000-year-old kitchen cupboard.

Fitted Kitchens

At Skara Brae, in the Orkney Islands off Scotland, a group of stone houses survives from 5,000 years ago. Each home has a hearth at its centre. One house has a watertight stone bowl, probably used to hold shellfish. Tools called querns were used to grind flour. The stone cupboards round the walls once held kitchen equipment and food.

Smoky Baking

▶ In this tomb painting from 1400 BC, Egyptian cooks are plucking ducks, then filling them with salt to preserve them.

Mummy's Home Cooking

We know that the cooking of the ancient Egyptians was very smoky, because soot has been found in the lungs of many mummies. To avoid this smoke, people cooked on the flat roofs of houses or in open-air kitchens. Because meat went off quickly in the heat, ordinary Egyptian people lived mainly on vegetables such as peas, beans and lentils. They mixed crushed chickpeas with sesame-seed oil to make hummus, which is still popular today.

▼ This model of an Egyptian kitchen from about 1900 BC shows cooks grinding flour, kneading dough and baking loaves.

Ancient Egyptian bread came in little triangular buns called *ta*. These were baked in small, cone-shaped ovens made from Nile mud, with manure or rotten vegetables for fuel. Out in the country, people baked bread in the ashes of their open fires.

Ancient Grease

Healthy eaters might admire the diet of the ancient Greeks. They ate porridge and bread rather than red meat, and avoided fat. Country people kept goats and hens for milk, cheese and eggs. Figs, fish and olives (eaten raw or pressed into olive oil) were on the menu almost every day. For breakfast, the Greeks had freshly baked bread dipped in wine. A wine strainer was an essential piece of kitchen equipment.

▲ A model, made 2,500 years ago, showing ancient Greek bread-making.

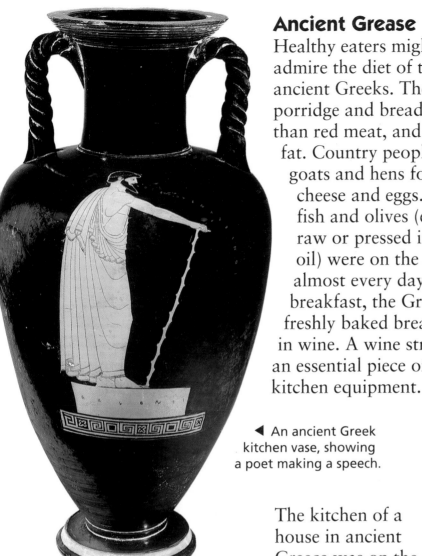

◄ An ancient Greek kitchen vase, showing a poet making a speech.

The kitchen of a house in ancient Greece was on the ground floor, next to an open courtyard. All the cooking was done on an open wood fire, built on a platform in the middle of the kitchen. It must have been a scorchingly hot place to work for the women who had to prepare all the meals. Only the biggest homes had the luxury of a chimney.

TASTY TITBITS

Rare Treats
The historian Herodotus says of the ancient Egyptian diet: 'Of course, various birds, quails, duck and small fowl are pickled and eaten uncooked.'

FANCY THAT!

A Woman's Place
The poet on the vase, above, may have been talking about the sexes. Ancient Greek homes were strictly divided into men's and women's areas. The kitchen was, of course, in the women's quarters!

Spicy Stories

Culinary Delights

The word 'culinary' comes from the Latin *culina*, which means kitchen. The culina of a Roman villa was well-equipped with brick-lined ovens, cooking implements and storage jars like those in the picture below.

TASTY TITBITS

Potty Romans
Cheap Roman pots absorbed strong flavours, which passed into the next dish that was cooked in them. Some recipes by Roman cookery writer Apicius began: 'Take a new pot ...'

▲ A Roman beaker.

Roman people liked strong flavours. As well as spices, they used a sharp sauce called *liquamen* which was made in Spain from rotting fish. Mix together a dash of Tabasco with a teaspoon of Worcester Sauce and you will get some idea of its taste. Beware – it is powerful stuff!

▼ A reconstructed Roman kitchen, with a charcoal stove. The jars propped against the wall contained olive oil, wine and liquamen.

Public Kitchens

Poor Romans lived in tall apartment blocks called *insulae*, which means 'islands'. Their small flats had no space for a kitchen. Instead, all the families in each *insula* shared one large public kitchen. But Roman towns had so many bakeries and market stalls selling hot snacks, that it was often easier to buy your food already cooked.

In country villas, slaves did the kitchen chores for rich Romans. They cooked on charcoal stoves, which were like modern barbecues. These were placed under windows, so the fumes could escape. At a Roman villa in Rockbourne, Hampshire, archaeologists have found the remains of a self-closing kitchen door. The owners must have wanted to keep cooking smells out of the other rooms.

FANCY THAT!

Mousetrap
Rich Romans considered dormouse a delicacy. Mice were specially fattened for the pot. In the kitchen they were slit open, and stuffed with minced beef or the meat of other mice. They were then sewn up and cooked. Delicious!

▲ This Roman implement, called a *mortarium*, was used for grinding hard spices such as pepper.

▲ A third-century mosaic of a slave carrying cooked dishes from the kitchen.

9

Hearth Burn

Saxon Stews

As they waved goodbye to the Romans in AD 410, the British people probably gave little thought to their stomachs. Within a few years, they had forgotten exotic Roman tastes. The Saxon invaders who soon arrived built homes without separate kitchens. They had just one room, with a hearth burning constantly at its centre. Over the fire, stews called 'pottages', containing meat, vegetables and grain, were slowly boiled in large, iron cauldrons.

▲ A reconstructed Viking house, with its central hearth. Stores hang from the ceiling, safe from rats.

▼ The Saxons made drinking vessels from animal horns.

TASTY TITBITS

A King in the Kitchen
Alfred the Great, English king from 871 to 899, was once resting in a peasant woman's cottage before a battle. She had left some cakes baking in the ashes round the fire, and Alfred did not notice them burning. The old woman returned and told the king off for not paying attention.

Viking Victuals

The Viking warriors who settled in Britain after the eighth century ate a lot of boiled or roast meats, especially bacon and mutton. 'Cauldron snake' was their name for a long, spiced sausage boiled in a pot. They also caught seagulls in nets and stewed them, though they were rather stringy and tough. Viking and Saxon bread would also seem chewy to us. Pounding grain to extract flour was a back-breaking task for women. Windmills were not invented until Norman times, so grinding flour was a daily kitchen chore.

FANCY THAT!

Food for Thought
If there was a bad harvest, the Vikings cooked food only for healthy members of the family. Children were fed, but the sick and elderly were left to starve.

◄ A reconstructed Viking larder in York. Meat and fish were salted, smoked or dried to preserve them for the long winter months. Dried fish is still popular in Scandinavia, where the Vikings came from.

▼ A raised hearth made cooking easier. Different foods could all be cooked together, in a big iron pot.

A Sunken Oven

The Vikings baked buns and oatcakes on a smooth stone heated in the fire. They cooked meat in ovens like those used in prehistoric times – pits packed with hot stones, then covered with leaves and earth to keep the heat in. The brick-lined baker's ovens of Roman towns had been forgotten.

A Medieval Mess

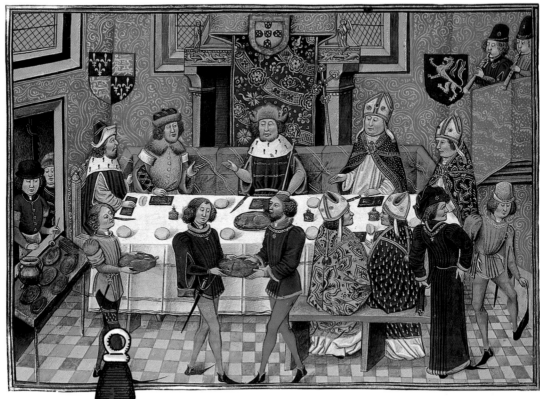

▲ Food was served through a hatchway for this feast in a wealthy medieval house.

TASTY TITBITS

A Medieval Rhyme
'Pease pottage hot,
Pease pottage cold,
Pease pottage
in the pot,
Nine days
old.'

A Buttery Taste

You probably do not cook your dinner in your hall or bedroom. But this was quite normal in the Middle Ages, when every room was used for many different purposes. Only in large houses, like the one shown above, was there a special kitchen. There were, though, separate rooms for storing food. The 'buttery' (*bouteille* is French for bottle) was for liquid foods. The 'pantry' (*pain* means bread in French) was for solids.

A Smoky Hall

Kitchen jobs such as preparing and cooking food were commonly done in the hall of a medieval house. This was the main room of the house, also used for working, eating and sleeping. Smoke from the log fire at its centre found its way out through windows or holes in the roof. Windows, at this time, did not have any glass.

Table Manners

Medieval people were very particular about mealtime manners. They did not use plates, but ate off slices of stale bread called 'trenchers'. At least it saved washing up. Only after the meal were you allowed to throw your trencher on the floor for the dogs. Blowing your nose on the tablecloth was frowned upon. 'Courtesy Books' also advised against removing your hat at table, as the lice might drop out of your hair into the food.

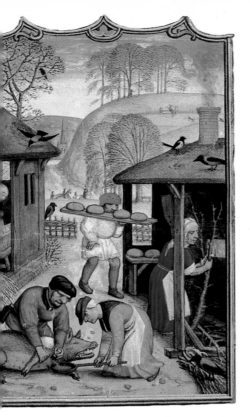

▲ Fifteenth-century cooks at work. One woman heats the oven, while another kneads dough. Outside, the people killing the pig save its blood to make black puddings.

▶ When meat was roasted on spits, pans collected the fatty drips. This 'dripping' was used to make soap and candles.

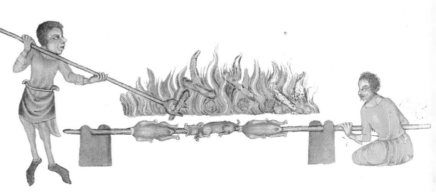

Another Fine Mess

No doubt some medieval folk were messy eaters, but they all ate a mess! A 'mess' was the name for a serving of food shared by four people. Often it was a mess of rich pottage, containing wild birds as well as farmed meat. For the poor, a mess was likely to contain cabbages, onions and leeks boiled up with animal heads, bones and offal.

13

Middle Age Spreads

Castle Kitchens

In castles in the Middle Ages, the soldiers' food was normally prepared outside in the open 'bailey' area. But this was not safe if the castle was under attack. Instead, a stone turret or staircase was used as an emergency kitchen fireplace. A well within it provided fresh water.

The picture on the right shows a rich lord's kitchen from the 1400s. The fire burns under a chimney. This was much less smoky than the Saxons' open fire in the middle of the room. Even so, kitchen work remained hot and dirty. Notice the cook's apron, which protected his clothes from soot and grease.

▶ A cook in the Middle Ages, preparing his lord's dinner.

FANCY THAT!
Cutting Remarks
Medieval 'books of carving' told cooks how to prepare meats. Directions included how to 'dismember a heron', 'lift a swan', 'unbrace a duck' and 'slat a pike'. Most creatures were on the medieval menu, even 'four and twenty blackbirds baked in a pie'.

▶ We can still visit the medieval kitchen at Glastonbury Abbey, in Somerset.

▲ Herb gardens were just outside the monastery kitchen. Here, the monks grew 'pot herbs' for flavouring food, and others for medicines, dyes and perfuming rooms.

Holy Orders

Medieval monasteries had large numbers of mouths to feed – not just monks, but workers, guests and beggars. Their kitchens had to be large and well-planned. The abbot's kitchen at the abbey in Glastonbury had a huge hearth. It was in a separate, stone building to reduce the risk of fire. On festival days, monks ate pork pies, fig tarts and a 'pittance' – an extra helping of fruit or cheese.

The monastery kitchen was next to the refectory, where the monks ate. They did not want food to get cold on its way to the table. Cellars and storerooms were close by, and a door led to the kitchen garden. The monks grew fresh vegetables and herbs, especially onions, leeks and garlic.

▶ This cook appears in *The Canterbury Tales*, written by Geoffrey Chaucer in the 1380s. Notice his special hook for hanging pots over a fire.

Meaty Matters

▲ A wide variety of meat was carefully prepared for sale in a sixteenth-century butcher's shop.

Seasoned Meat

You can buy almost any food in a modern supermarket whatever the time of year. Meat and fish stay fresh for years when frozen, and can be eaten in any season. But in Tudor and Stuart times, fresh meat in winter was a luxury. Farmers butchered animals as soon as the grass stopped growing. During the autumn, kitchens were busy with people cutting up meat and packing it in barrels full of salt to preserve it. Old or 'tainted' meat was buried with charcoal to improve its taste. People also disguised the flavour of old meat by cooking it with strong herbs and spices.

TASTY TITBITS

Early Birds
Thomas Tusser advised Elizabeth housewives to get up at 5 am, to be sure of finishing all their jobs on time. He said that early rising also set a good example to their maids.

◀ A Tudor kitchen at Compton Castle, in Devon. The fireplace was wide enough for several pots and spits. A shelf in the wall was used for storing salt, so that it would not get damp.

Chimney Stock

If you look up a Tudor kitchen chimney, you will probably see some iron hooks. Meat and fish were hung on these and 'smoked'. To make the meat taste pleasant, only the best sort of smoke would do. Throwing the bark and sawdust of oak trees on the fire gave off thick clouds of sweet-smelling smoke. This stopped the food going rotten, and gave it a strong flavour. Many people still enjoy kippers (smoked herring) and smoked bacon.

FANCY THAT!

Sole Food
Tudor women wore clogs called 'pattens', with iron rings on the soles to raise their feet above the filthy kitchen floor. Those who went barefoot were said to be 'slip shod'.

A Sweet Smile

For banquets, cooks prepared colourful dishes in amusing shapes. As sugar became more readily available, sweet dishes with jelly and 'marchpane' (marzipan) became very popular. Queen Elizabeth I's teeth turned black from eating too much sugar!

▶ A selection of Tudor sweets.

Fit for a King

▲ A sixteenth-century cook making pies. The tradition of mince pies at Christmas began in Tudor times with minced-meat pies.

Beastly Feasts

At a banquet in Greenwich, King Henry VIII once feasted for seven hours without a break. An Italian guest noted how kitchen servants brought out dishes of 'every sort of meat known in the kingdom'. The meal ended with twenty jellies, 'made in the shape of castles and animals of various descriptions as beautiful as can be imagined'. Eating rich foods, like dressing in fine clothes, showed a person's importance.

TASTY TITBITS

Pepys in the Oven
'Found my wife making of pies and tarts to try her oven with. But not knowing the nature of it, did heat it too hot, and so a little overbake her things, but knows how to do it better another time.' (Diary of Samuel Pepys)

When Henry visited the Marquess of Exeter in 1533, the menu included duck, gulls, sparrows, gannet, heron, chickens, quail, partridge, rabbits and venison. No wonder the king became so fat, at one time measuring 145 cm round his chest.

18

Baking Classes

Do you prefer brown or white bread? In Tudor and Stuart times, top-quality flour was sifted, or 'bolted', through linen to remove the dark bran. Bread made from this flour was called 'white', but was really cream-coloured. The different classes ate different types of bread. The weekly bake in the kitchen of a big house included white buns called 'manchets' for the rich, coarse brown loaves called 'cockets' for servants, and hard, black 'tourte' for farm workers.

FANCY THAT!

Midnight Feasts
Tudor and Stuart cooks prepared snacks called 'liveries' for bedside 'livery cupboards'. If you woke up feeling peckish, you simply raided the cupboard!

◀ Hampton Court kitchens, which had many huge ovens to prepare great feasts for Henry VIII.

▼ The Tudors used plates rather than trenchers of bread. The rich ate off silver, the middle classes pewter (below, from Little Moreton Hall) and the poor from wooden bowls.

The Well-laid Table

In 1595, staff served Lord Montague's dinner guests with great ceremony. A trumpet sounded, and the kitchen servants entered in a procession. The 'yeoman usher' kissed his lordship's hand, then directed the laying of the tablecloths. The 'yeomen of the pantry' placed plates, bread rolls and silver cutlery before each diner, bowing twice as they did so. The carvers and table servants washed their hands publicly. Then, everyone stood in silence as the dishes of food were carried in. The meats were set before his lordship, and the carving could begin.

The Art of Cookery

Desperate Measures

A good cook needs accurate kitchen scales. But in the Georgian kitchen, they were not much use. Recipes rarely showed quantities. If they did, it was 'a bit of this – a handful of that – a sprinkle of salt and a shake of pepper'. In *The Art of Cookery Made Plain and Easy*, published in 1747, Hannah Glasse tried to be more precise. She described how to prepare French-style dishes, but admitted that one of her recipes for partridge was just 'an odd jumble of trash'.

▲ A detail from a seventeenth-century painting of a woman frying eggs. Some recipes never change.

Hot Dogs

The Georgian passion for eating meat brought some ingenious inventions. Large joints were roasted on spits in front of the fire. Some spits were operated by a fan in the chimney. This was rotated by the heat of the fire and connected by pulleys to the spit. Other spits were turned by small dogs or geese walking in a treadwheel.

▶ 'Turnspit' dogs were trained for the job. Perhaps they got scraps as a reward.

Coal Comfort

In the 1700s, coal was becoming cheap and readily available. Gradually, people began to abandon their great log fires and install raised iron grates called 'kitcheners'. These were much better suited to burning coal.

▼ The well-equipped Georgian kitchens at the Royal Pavilion, in Brighton.

▲ This 'hastener' saved time when roasting meat. The central hook was rotated by clockwork.

Narrower coal fires had space on either side of the grate for brick or iron hotplates. Cooks now used these to prepare small side dishes. Potatoes were boiled 'in their shells [skins]'. Small copper pans used to heat sauces were given the name 'saucepans'.

In some places, change was slower. Some Scottish Highland families still boiled their food in animal skins turned inside out. They dropped hot stones into the water to make it boil, just as their Stone Age ancestors had done.

TASTY TITBITS

A Soup Opera
'If a lump of soot falls in the soup, stir it in well for a high French flavour ... If dinner is late, put the clock back, and then it may be ready in a minute.'
(Jonathan Swift's *Advice to Servants*, 1745)

FANCY THAT!

Cooking your Goose Georgian recipes included one for a 'self-roasting goose'. It was plucked then made to run round the fire until it dropped, exhausted and well done.

Home On the Range

The Smoky Monster

As Victoria was crowned queen in 1837, the nation's kitchens prepared for change. Cooks were installing big, iron 'ranges', which had to be polished daily with black lead. Despite occasional belches of smoke, they were more efficient than open fires. By 1901, hardly a kitchen in the land had not been affected by the new technology of Victorian times.

▲ Knives rusted unless they were polished, with brick powder or a cleaning machine like this one.

◀ By 1850, even small homes had a range like this, with an oven and hotplates.

FANCY THAT!
Antique Stew
Food was first sealed in tin cans in 1812, by the London firm of Donkin and Hall. A tin of their veal and carrot stew made in 1818 was opened in 1938. The contents were still perfectly edible.

Cook's Chores

Do you help in the kitchen? Well-off Victorian families had servants to do their dirty jobs. 'Cook' prepared food while a scullery maid pumped water, scrubbed floors and washed dishes. The maid's working hours were very long, from 6.30 am (when she lit the range) to 10.30 pm (when she dried the last dinner plate). Lift a Victorian iron cooking pot to discover how strong you needed to be to work in the kitchen.

▲ The walls of this Victorian kitchen at Lanhydrock, Cornwall, were painted blue to scare away flies.

▲ Kitchen staff enjoy a break from their duties, but the mistress approaches.

What the Butler Saw

Most Victorian maids led a fairly lonely life working on their own in small homes, cleaning, cooking and waiting at table. But in a grand house, life as a servant could be much more fun. Many girls began as kitchen maids but rose through the ranks to become well-paid cooks. Very rich families sometimes had a butler as well as a cook. The butler's pantry was like his private office, where all the valuable cutlery, silver and glasses were stored.

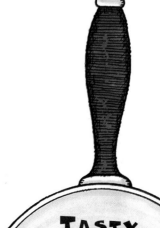

TASTY TITBITS

Dressing the Chicken
'Cook gave me a chicken and told me to dress it. I found some paper pie frills, and put one on each leg and one round the neck. You can imagine the look on cook's face. She'd expected me to pluck it!'
(A Victorian maid)

Triumphs of Technology

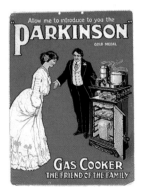

▲ By 1860, gas cookers had a modern design – burners on top, oven beneath.

A Gas Explosion

By 1901, nearly all kitchens had a range of some sort, however small. Cooking, heating and lighting were powered by gas in many towns. Gas cookers, although sold as early as 1830, had been slow to catch on. People were frightened of explosions, and claimed that gas gave their food a nasty taste. But they were a big improvement in kitchen technology. By 1880, gas companies were renting out cookers to poor families. Some installed coin-in-the-slot meters, so that cookers could be used without running up huge bills.

▲ Roasting a goose in a large coal range. The hidden fire of this 'closed range' was less wasteful than earlier 'open fire' designs.

TASTY TITBITS

A Clean Kitchen
'Scrub out the larder twice a week ... Clear up as you go. Muddle makes more muddle ... A dirty kitchen is a disgrace to both mistress and maid.'
(Mrs Beeton, 1861)

▲ Victorian kitchen appliances.

On the Shelf

If you could peep into a pantry of 1900, you might find as many packets as today. Tins, jars and packs of ready-made foods saved housewives a lot of work. Colman's English Mustard (1846), Heinz Baked Beans (1875), Jacob's Cream Crackers (1885), Oxo Cubes (1890) and Corn Flakes (1898) were soon firm favourites.

▼ Packaged foods had colourful labels to catch the eye.

▼ One of Mrs Beeton's famous cookery books.

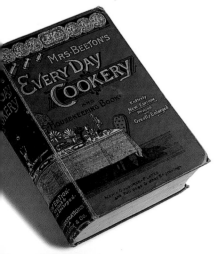

Cooking the Books

As a young wife, Mrs Isabella Beeton was appalled by the sloppy kitchens of her middle-class neighbours. 'There is no more fruitful source of family discontent,' she said, 'than a housewife's badly cooked dinners and untidy ways.' To help them, she began writing magazine articles with recipes and practical tips. In 1861, these appeared as the *Book of Household Management*. By 1900, there was a copy in almost every kitchen in Britain. It is still on sale today.

The Daily Drudge

Safe to Drink?

Until the 1880s, many homes had no piped water. People had to queue at public pumps with buckets and jugs. Some houses had their own wells and pumps in the garden, or even indoors in the scullery. But the water often contained sewage from leaky cesspits.

Scullery Skivvies

What is your most hated kitchen job? Scrubbing pans? Peeling potatoes? A Victorian servant or 'skivvy' did these chores in the 'scullery'. This room had a stone sink which grazed the knuckles and a wooden washing-up bowl full of splinters. There was no washing-up liquid – you just scrubbed with sand and soda. It removed the grease, but left the skivvy with raw fingers.

▲ This Victorian water purifier used charcoal to filter out dirt.

▲ Copper pans at Lanhydrock, Cornwall. They had to be cleaned regularly with vinegar and silver sand.

TASTY TITBITS

A Bright Copper
'Every copper stewpan and saucepan must be kept bright without and well-tinned within,' said the *Housekeeper's Guide*. Copper pans were lined with tin to prevent poisoning.

High Tea

Near the Victorian scullery, was a pantry for storing food. This was usually on the cold, north-facing side of the house, with tiled walls and slate shelves for keeping meat cool. Some strange substances were found in the pantry. Cheating bakers added chalk or ground-up bones to flour, to make their bread heavier. Grocers mixed sand with sugar. Milk was often watered down. Tea leaves sometimes had sloe leaves (which are poisonous), gunpowder or sheep's dung added to them.

FANCY THAT!

The PM's Tea.
William Gladstone, the famous Victorian Prime Minister, loved nothing better than a cup of strong tea. He even filled his hot water bottle with tea so that he could go to sleep warming his feet on his favourite drink.

▲ A Victorian icebox. Ice in the top slowly melts, chilling the food as it does so. The tap is for draining off water.

Locked-in Flavour

On their 'at home' days, Victorian ladies invited their friends round for afternoon tea and freshly baked scones. Cook baked the scones, but servants were not trusted to make tea. The maid's job was simply to keep the tea urn full of boiling water. The caddy holding the precious tea leaves was kept locked, and only the mistress knew where to find the key.

▲ The daily drudge was broken by a visit to the fair, where these men roast an ox in about 1890.

The Flick of a Switch

The Ideal Home

Over the centuries, the race to improve the kitchen had hotted up. Between 1930 and 1960, there was a kitchen revolution that affected everyone. Middle-class families could no longer afford to pay cooks and maids. Servants lost their jobs, and kitchens suffered. People no longer had time to disinfect the larder twice a week, as Mrs Beeton recommended.

The rapid spread of electricity allowed people to turn to labour-saving devices – toasters, fridges, mixers and dishwashers. In 1918, only six per cent of homes had electricity. By 1949, this figure had risen to eighty-six per cent.

FANCY THAT !

Whale Meat Again
In wartime, people ate strange things, like egg powder, marrow jam and 'snoek' (dried whale meat). The author's parents casseroled Snowy, their pet rabbit!

◀ During the Second World War, people used ration books when buying food.

▼ When London's gas was cut off in 1940, Mr Price, a baker, cooked meals for three pence.

WHAT YOU CAN'T COOK, WE CAN BRING YOUR DINNER HERE TO BE COOKED. 3D PER Co.

A Brighter Future

What would the Victorians have made of the kitchen in this 1957 advert (left)? It may not be very cosy, but it is certainly much brighter and neater than their kitchens! All the units are designed to fit together, with easy-to-clean surfaces and no gaps where dirt might collect. This housewife does all her own kitchen chores. She would never accept the gloomy room at the back of the house, or below ground in a basement, that her Victorian grandmother had cooked in.

TV Dinners

One of the first BBC Radio broadcasts in 1927 was called 'Planning an Ideal Kitchen'. Before long, millions of people got their cookery tips from the radio. During the Second World War, a daily, five-minute cookery programme called 'The Kitchen Front' gave advice on how to make 'square meals' from rationed ingredients. Since the 1950s, television chefs from Fanny Cradock to Delia Smith have cooked in studio kitchens. 'Here's one I made earlier' has become a popular kitchen catchphrase.

FORMICA* for me!

Smart housewives love formica laminated plastic. It's a joy in the kitchen, because it won't stain, crack or chip, resists heat up to 310°F. and is wiped clean with a damp cloth.

And now formica surfaces have made themselves at home all over the house, in the most elegant surroundings. Dining tables, cocktail cabinets, coffee tables, easily cleaned storage shelves. formica laminated plastic is right wherever you put it.

Price. For as little as 35/- you can cover a table 3 ft. x 2 ft. including De La Rue's own Domestic Adhesive. And formica laminated plastic wears and looks beautiful for a lifetime.

Write for full colour leaflet to Thomas De La Rue & Co Ltd, Dept. 205A, 84/86 Regent Street, London W1

Look for the FORMICA name on every sheet!

*Formica is the registered name for the laminated plastic made by Thomas De La Rue & Co Ltd.

▲ Formica plastic kitchen surfaces came in bright, bold colours.

TASTY TITBITS

Off Your Trolley
'If you happen to be the proud possessor of a heated trolley, everything hot can be slipped into this, with cold items on the bottom shelf. This enables the cook-hostess, as well as everyone else, to watch the television.'
(Fanny Cradock, 1970)

▼ Modern stainless-steel saucepans have non-stick surfaces that do not require hours of scouring and polishing.

COOKING TIMES

3000 BC	Farming begins in Britain.
	The first permanent homes with kitchens are built.
600 BC	Iron knives and cooking pots are first used in Britain.
AD 43	The Romans conquer Britain, and introduce charcoal stoves.
AD 300	Apicius writes his Roman cookery book.
AD 410	Saxons invade England. Cooks use central log fires.
AD 1066	Outdoor kitchens are built in Norman castles.
AD 1120	Windmills are used for grinding flour.
AD 1200	Monasteries are built with large separate kitchen buildings.
AD 1319	The first recorded sales of sugar in Britain.
AD 1400	Town houses have separate kitchens to reduce risk of fires.
AD 1530	Corks are first used to seal bottles.
AD 1600	Kitchen chimneys are common as bricks become cheaper.
AD 1660	Forks are coming into use in Britain.
AD 1790	The first iron cooking ranges are manufactured.
AD 1812	The first tinned food is produced, by Donkin and Hall.
AD 1830	Gas cookers go on sale.
AD 1861	Mrs Beeton's *Book of Household Management* is published.
AD 1875	Tinned baked beans go on sale.
AD 1886	Bovril and Coca-Cola 'brain tonic' are introduced.
AD 1889	The electric cooker is invented.
AD 1920	Stainless-steel kitchen implements are introduced.
AD 1923	Electric refrigerators go on sale.
AD 1927	The first radio cookery programme is broadcast.
AD 1940	Food rationing begins because of the Second World War.
AD 1953	Food rationing ends.
AD 1965	The microwave oven is invented.

PLACES TO VISIT

Corinium Museum, Cirencester, Gloucestershire. Tel: 01285 655611
Reconstructed Roman kitchen with displays of cooking equipment.

Hampton Court Palace, London. Tel: 0181 781 9500
Many a royal feast was prepared in the vast Tudor kitchens built in 1514.

Jorvik Centre, York, Yorkshire. Tel: 01904 643211
Take a ride through reconstructed Viking kitchens with real cooking smells.

Kentwell Hall, Long Melford, Suffolk. Tel: 01787 310207
The kitchens of this Tudor mansion are brought to life for 'living history' events.

Llancaiach Fawr, near Cardiff, Wales. Tel: 01443 412248
You can help with kitchen chores at this living history museum of life in the 1640s.

The People's Story, Edinburgh, Scotland. Tel: 0131 529 4057
A glimpse into the home life of ordinary people in the recent past.

GLOSSARY

Appliances	Machines and equipment
Archaeologists	People who study history through ancient remains
Bailey	A court enclosed by a castle's outer wall
Black puddings	Thick sausages made from animals' blood
Bolted	Sieved through a coarse cloth
Caddy	A small box containing tea
Cauldrons	Large, deep, bowl-shaped cooking vessels
Cesspits	Drainage pits for toilet waste
Culinary	To do with the kitchen
Dough	A lump of moist, kneaded flour
Fertile	Producing large amounts of fruit or crops
Grate	A metal framework over the fuel in a fireplace
Hearth	The floor or front of a fireplace
Heron	A large, wading bird
Kneading	Squeezing and pressing flour to make dough
Middle Ages	The period of European history from AD 1000 to 1453
Mortarium	A bowl used for crushing spices with a pestle
Pike	A large, freshwater fish
Quern	A large stone used for crushing grain to make flour
Ranges	Large stoves, in which the oven is kept constantly hot
Refectory	The large dining hall in a monastery or school
Scullery	A small kitchen room for washing up
Skivvy	A servant who does all the worst jobs
Spit	A spike or skewer on which food is roasted
Stone Age	Prehistoric period when tools were made from stone
Treadwheel	A wheel turned by foot to power something
Victuals	Food, provisions
Villas	Large Roman country houses, with estates
Yeoman	A middle-class man

  # BOOKS TO READ

Black, M. *The Medieval Cookbook* (British Museum, 1993)

Chrisp, P. *Tudors and Stuarts – Food* (Wayland, 1994)

Corbishley, G. *Appetite for Change* (English Heritage, 1993)

Davies, J. *The Victorian Kitchen* (BBC Books, 1989)

Faulkner, L. *Victorian Kitchens* (Wayland, 1993)

Ventura, P. *Food Through the Ages* (Macdonald Young Books, 1994)

Wood, R. *History of Food and Cooking* (Wayland, 1996)

INDEX